EAST RIDING
OF YORKSHIRE COUNCIL

Schools Library Service

PROJECT
April 2013

www.heinemannlibrary.co.uk
Visit our website to find out more
information about Heinemann
Library books.

To order:
☎ Phone +44 (0) 1865 888066
🖨 Fax +44 (0) 1865 314091
🖳 Visit www.heinemannlibrary.co.uk

Heinemann Library is an imprint of **Capstone Global Library Limited**, a company incorporated in England and Wales having its registered office at 7 Pilgrim Street, London, EC4V 6LB – Registered company number: 6695582

"Heinemann Library" is a registered trademark of Pearson Education Limited, under licence to Capstone Global Library Limited

Written by Lynette Evans
Edited by Briony Hill
Designed by Avon Willis
Original illustrations © Weldon Owen Education Inc. 2008
Illustrated by Amy Lam
Picture research by Jamshed Mistry
Originated by Weldon Owen Education Inc.

Printed in China through Colorcraft Ltd., Hong Kong

Acknowledgements
We would like to thank the following for permission to reproduce photographs: Getty Images (bear on melting ice, pp. 14–15; Mount Kilimanjaro, p. 20); Jennifer and Brian Lupton (girl, p. 22); Stockbyte (girl, p. 23); Tranz/Corbis (cover; pp. 1–14; scientist and bear cub, p.15; pp. 16–19; glacier, storm, p. 20; p. 21; p. 24)

ISBN 978-0-431179-67-4 (hardback)
13 12 11 10 09
10 9 8 7 6 5 4 3 2 1

British Library Cataloguing in Publication Data
Evans, Lynette.
  On thin ice: climate change. – (Worldscapes)
551.6-dc22
A full catalogue record for this book is available from the British Library.

Every effort has been made to contact copyright holders of material reproduced in this book. Any omissions will be rectified in subsequent printings if notice is given to the publishers.

Disclaimer
All the Internet addresses (URLs) given in this book were valid at the time of going to press. However, due to the dynamic nature of the Internet, some addresses may have changed, or sites may have changed or ceased to exist since publication. While the author and Publishers regret any inconvenience this may cause readers, no responsibility for any such changes can be accepted by either the author or the Publishers.

On Thin Ice

Written by Lynette Evans
Illustrated by Amy Lam

Arctic

My name is Anana. I live in Churchill, northern Canada. Each year in October, hundreds of polar bears gather by the sea. They wait for Hudson Bay to freeze so they can hunt seals from the ice. This October, the water has not yet frozen over. What will the bears do?

Contents

Look for the **Thinking Cap**.
When you see this picture, you will find
a problem to think about and write about.

On thin ice

First steps

It is spring. Littlest Bear sniffs the cold, white snow.
He blinks in the bright sunlight. His sister is already
playing outside. Littlest Bear can see his mother's
huge footprints. He wants to follow them. It is time
to leave the den. Littlest Bear is **determined**.
He takes one step, then another, and another.

determined to have made up your mind to do something no matter what

Long walk

Mother Bear is hungry. She has **fasted** for almost eight months. She takes her cubs on a long walk to the sea. Littlest Bear works hard to keep up. He is smaller than Sister Bear. He struggles against the icy wind. Littlest Bear is glad when his mother stops.

She knows her cubs need to drink and rest. She knows her cubs want to roll and play. Mother Bear is tired too. She makes a day den in the snow.

fast to go without food

Female polar bears give birth to two or three cubs. The biggest cubs get more food. The smallest cub may not live.

Frozen sea

The bear cubs are bigger now. Littlest Bear
is still the weaker cub, but he has kept up.
Now they are at a big bay. A sheet of ice stretches
over the sea. Littlest Bear sniffs the salty air.

Mother Bear tests the new ice to be sure that
it is thick enough to walk on. Then she leads
her cubs out over the frozen sea. She is a strong
hunter. Seals are her **prey**. She must eat and
grow fat so that she can keep feeding her cubs.

prey animal that is hunted and eaten by another animal

Polar bear cubs drink their mother's milk until they are about two-and-a-half years old. Then they start to hunt and eat meat.

Meltdown

It is summer. The ice is becoming thinner.
Suddenly, it creaks and snaps. A chunk of ice
breaks away. Littlest Bear falls into the water.
He paddles with his paws. Like Sister Bear,
he knows how to swim. Mother Bear will
give him a ride on her back if he gets tired.

It is time for the bears to return to shore.
The sea ice is melting early. Mother Bear can
no longer hunt for seals. She will not eat until
cold weather comes and the water freezes again.

Polar bears are strong swimmers. They can swim a long way if they have to, but they need to rest on the ice.

Watching and waiting

It is autumn. The nights are long and cold. Littlest Bear walks by his mother's side. She is thinner now, but her cubs have grown. The first snow has fallen. A cold wind blows over the bay. It holds a promise of ice. Mother Bear may soon hunt and feed again.

Mother Bear takes her cubs to the edge of the **tundra**. They gather with many other bears and look out over the bay. They watch for the thick ice to come. The bears wait and wait and w a i t ...

tundra ground that is frozen almost all year long

Write down your thoughts so that you can talk about these questions with a classmate.

1. What do you think might happen to the bears if the winter is not cold enough for the water to freeze?

2. Do you think people should be concerned about the Arctic ice melting? Why or why not?

3. Do you think there is anything people could do to help the bears? If so, what?

What's the issue?

Polar bears live in the Arctic. They hunt seals from the ice that forms over the sea. Scientists have been observing the polar bears. They say that polar bears are in trouble. Winters are becoming warmer in parts of the Arctic. The sea ice is breaking up earlier. It is forming later. Polar bears are losing the ice they need for hunting. They are going hungry and growing thin. Fewer cubs are **surviving**.

ARCTIC CIRCLE

Alaska (USA)

CANADA

RUSSIA

North Pole

GREENLAND

ARCTIC OCEAN

NORWAY

Some scientists predict that if the ice continues to melt in the Arctic, polar bears may die out by 2040.

survive to stay alive

14

This scientist holds a polar bear cub. The cub's mother is being fitted with an ear tag so scientists can keep track of her.

The bear facts

- Polar bears are the giants of the bear family. They are the largest **predators** on land.

- Polar bears must build up fat to survive through summer and autumn, when there is less food.

- Polar bears build up fat by feeding on seals in winter and spring. The earlier the ice melts in summer and the later it forms in autumn, the less time the bears have to hunt.

- If a mother polar bear is thin, she can't feed her cubs milk.

predator   animal that hunts and eats other animals

Feeling the heat

People living in the town of Churchill in northern Canada are noticing some big changes – big, white, furry animal changes!

Churchill lies near Wapusk National Park. The park is home to hundreds of polar bears. People go on polar bear tours from Churchill.

Buses take them north to see wild polar bears. These days, more and more polar bears are coming into town. People say the ice has melted early. They say it is forming late.

The polar bears are hungry. They are looking for food. What has caused this change?

HUDSON BAY

Churchill

Wapusk
National Park

CANADA

Put on your thinking cap

Write down your thoughts so that you can talk about these questions with a classmate.

1. What could happen to people when hungry polar bears come too close?

2. What do you think could happen to polar bears?

3. How do you think the problem could be solved?

CHURCHILL WILDERNESS ENCOUNTER

POLAR BEAR TOUR BUS

Climate detectives

Earth's **climate** has always been changing. It has shifted from warm times to cool times and back again. These changes have usually happened slowly over thousands of years.

A great deal of evidence shows that Earth is now in a period of global warming. Some scientists believe that this time of warming is part of Earth's natural cycle. However, many scientists believe that it is happening faster because of human activities.

Scientists search for clues to climate change. Nature keeps records in many ways. People drill ice cores from ice sheets. Ice cores have faint bands like rings. These show the yearly snowfall. By counting the bands, scientists can estimate the age of the ice.

climate the usual weather in a place

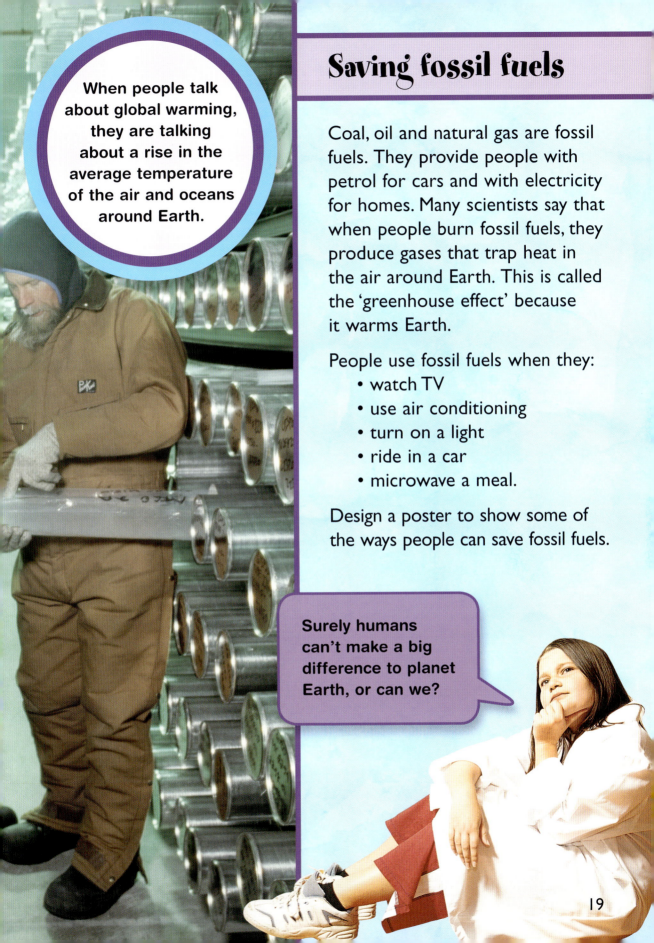

When people talk about global warming, they are talking about a rise in the average temperature of the air and oceans around Earth.

Saving fossil fuels

Coal, oil and natural gas are fossil fuels. They provide people with petrol for cars and with electricity for homes. Many scientists say that when people burn fossil fuels, they produce gases that trap heat in the air around Earth. This is called the 'greenhouse effect' because it warms Earth.

People use fossil fuels when they:
- watch TV
- use air conditioning
- turn on a light
- ride in a car
- microwave a meal.

Design a poster to show some of the ways people can save fossil fuels.

Surely humans can't make a big difference to planet Earth, or can we?

Hot spots around the world

Ice fields shrinking

PATAGONIA, ARGENTINA – Ice fields and glaciers are shrinking at an alarming rate. Many scientists say global warming is causing ice areas around the world to change.

Mountain snow melting

TANZANIA – Mount Kilimanjaro is the highest mountain in Africa. Its top is always covered with ice and snow. However, more than 80 per cent has melted since 1912.

Monster storm strikes

LOUISIANA, UNITED STATES – Sea levels are rising on Louisiana's southern coast. Hurricanes are becoming stronger. A hurricane gets its energy from warm water.

Nature's balance changing

MEXICO – The temperature affects whether sea turtles are male or female. Females hatch if the weather is warm. Males hatch if it is cold. Recently, scientists have recorded more female than male sea-turtle hatchlings.

Island disappearing

TUVALU, SOUTH PACIFIC – People who live on Tuvalu Island are losing their seaside homes. Sea levels are rising because of global warming. Families are having to move to nearby New Zealand.

Animals in danger

ANTARCTICA – The Adélie penguins of Antarctica depend on ice. They are disappearing from their normal homes around Antarctica. The sea ice is melting. The penguins have nowhere to go.

What's your opinion?

Scientists are working hard to answer some very important questions:

- Why are Arctic winters becoming warmer?
- Is the weather also changing in other places?
- How are plants and animals affected by the changes?
- What part do people play in the changing weather?

Scientists have gathered many facts over many years. Sometimes they agree, and sometimes they argue. What do you think about global warming?

Sometimes I think it would be nicer to have warmer weather, but now I realise that it can also be bad. A change in climate here can mean there's a change of climate in other places. Polar bears need ice, so a warmer world isn't good for them.

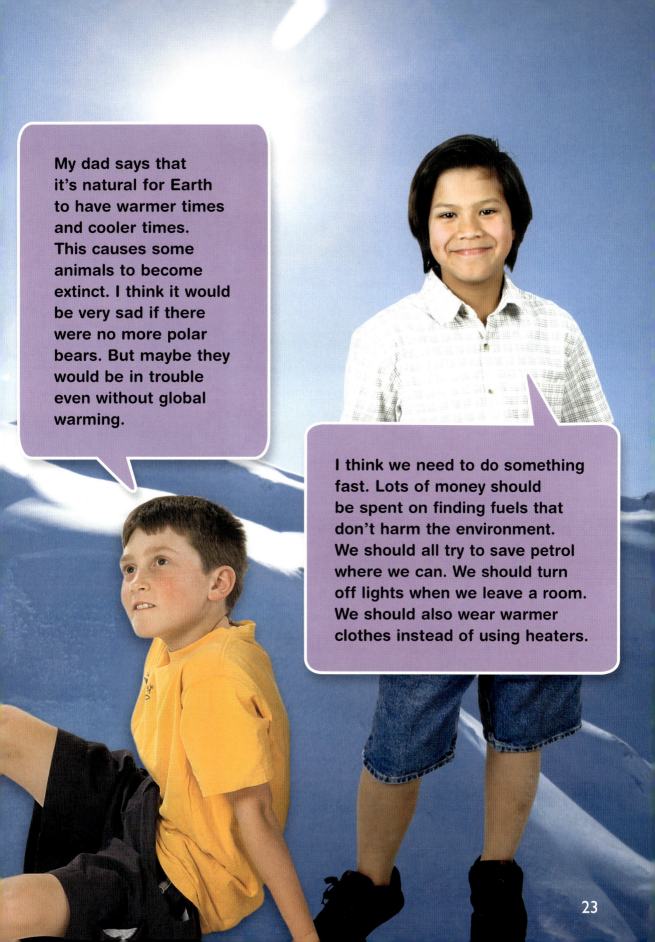

My dad says that it's natural for Earth to have warmer times and cooler times. This causes some animals to become extinct. I think it would be very sad if there were no more polar bears. But maybe they would be in trouble even without global warming.

I think we need to do something fast. Lots of money should be spent on finding fuels that don't harm the environment. We should all try to save petrol where we can. We should turn off lights when we leave a room. We should also wear warmer clothes instead of using heaters.

Think tank

1 What places and animals around the world are affected by global warming? What country or animal would you want to find out more about?

2 How do you think people, groups and countries could work together to reduce the amount of fossil fuels being used for energy?

Do your own research at the library, on the Internet, or with a parent or teacher to find out more about different viewpoints on global warming and how people are working to address the issues.

Glossary

climate the usual weather in a place

determined to have made up your mind to do something no matter what

fast to go without food

predator animal that hunts and eats other animals

prey animal that is hunted and eaten by another animal

survive to stay alive

tundra ground that is frozen almost all year long

Index